B♭ JAZZ

FOR TRUMPET, CLARINET & TENOR SAXOPHONE

ARRANGED BY SCOTT MCDONALD

PMI   **PROFESSIONAL MUSIC INSTITUTE** LLC
1336 Cruzero Street, Box 128, Ojai, CA 93024
info@promusicbooks.com

T0050708

FOR **TRUMPET, CLARINET** & **TENOR SAXOPHONE**

(The) Birth Of The Blues...**7**

Body And Soul...**6**

Cherry Pink And Apple Blossom White...**7**

Close Your Eyes...**8**

Crazy She Calls Me...**9**

(A) Day In The Life Of A Fool (Manha De Carnaval)...**10**

Deep Purple...**11**

Don't Get Around Much Anymore...**12**

Don't Worry 'Bout Me...**13**

For All We Know...**14**

Hang On Sloopy...**15**

How Little We Know...**16**

I Ain't Got Nothin' But The Blues...**18**

I Didn't Know About You...**17**

I'll Be Seeing You...**20**

I'm Beginning To See The Light...**21**

It All Depends On You...**22**

It Had To Be You...**23**

I've Got The World On A String...**24**

Let's Stay Together...**25**

Love Story...**45**

FOR **TRUMPET, CLARINET** & **TENOR SAXOPHONE**

Mood Indigo...26

Moonlight In Vermont...............................27

My Buddy..28

Perdido...29

Shiny Stockings.......................................30

Stormy Weather.......................................32

Sweet And Lovely....................................31

Taking A Chance On Love.........................34

Teach Me Tonight....................................35

That Sunday, That Summer........................36

There Will Never Be Another You................37

'Tis Autumn...38

Too Close For Comfort..............................39

We'll Be Together Again............................40

What Now My Love?.................................41

When Lights Are Low................................42

When You're Smiling.................................43

Where Are You?.......................................44

Where Do I Begin?...................................45

You Go To My Head.................................48

You Were Meant For Me............................46

The Birth Of The Blues

B♭ Instruments

Music by Ray Henderson
Lyric by B. G. DeSylva and Lew Brown

The birth of the blues 2-2

Body And Soul

Bb Instruments

Lyric by Edward Heyman, Robert Sour and Frank Eyton

Music by John Green

Cherry Pink And Apple Blossom White

B♭ Instruments

Music by Luis Guglielmi
Lyric by Mack David

Close Your Eyes

B♭ Instruments

Lyric and Music by
Bernice Petkere

Crazy She Calls Me

B♭ Instruments

Music by Carl Sigman
Lyric by Bob Russell

A Day In The Life Of A Fool
(Manha De Carnaval)

B♭ Instruments

Lyric by Carl Sigman
Music by Luiz Bonfa

Slowly, with a bossa nova beat

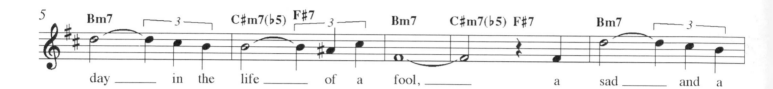

day _____ in the life _____ of a fool, _____ a sad _____ and a

long, _____ lone-ly day. _____ I walk the av - e-nue _____ and hope I'll

run in - to _____ the welcome sight of you _____ com-ing my way.

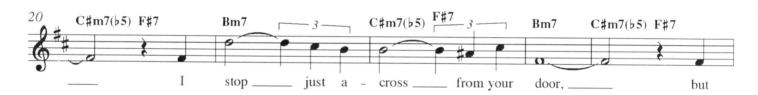

_____ I stop _____ just a - cross _____ from your door, _____ but

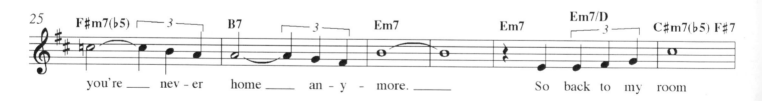

you're _____ nev - er home _____ an - y - more. _____ So back to my room

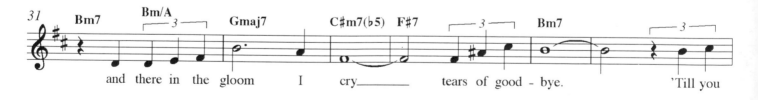

and there in the gloom I cry _____ tears of good - bye. 'Till you

Repeat and Fade

come back to me, that's the way it will be ev - 'ry day in the life of a fool. _____

Deep Purple

B♭ Instruments

Music by Peter De Rose
Lyric by Mitchell Parish

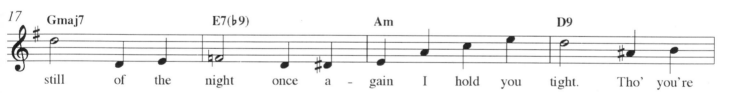

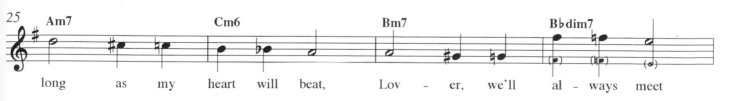

Don't Get Around Much Anymore

Bb Instruments

Music by Duke Ellington
Lyric by Bob Russell

Don't Worry 'Bout Me

B♭ Instruments

Music by Rube Bloom
Lyric by Ted Koehler

For All We Know

Music by J. Fred Coots
Lyric by Sam M. Lewis

Hang On Sloopy

B♭ Instruments

Lyric and Music by
Wes Farrell and Burt Russell

How Little We Know

(How Little It Matters)

Music by Phillip Springer
Lyric by Carolyn Leigh

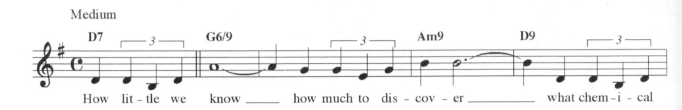

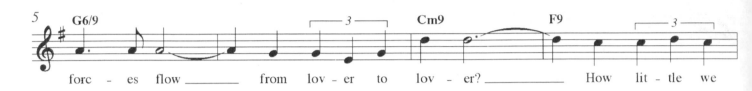

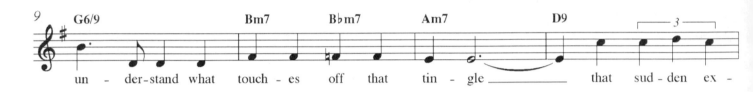

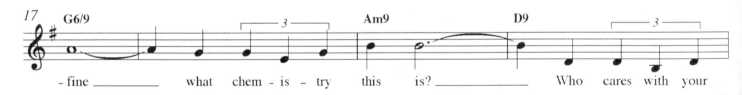

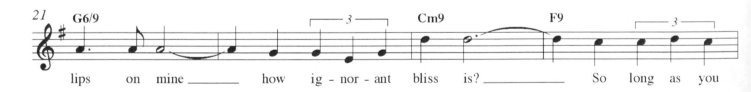

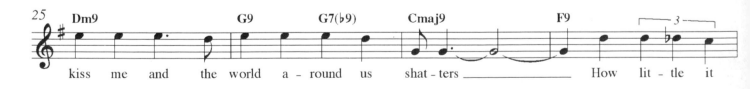

I Didn't Know About You

B♭ Instruments

Music by Duke Ellington
Lyric by Bob Russell

I Ain't Got Nothin' But The Blues

B♭ Instruments

Lyric by Don George and Larry Fotin
Music by Duke Ellington

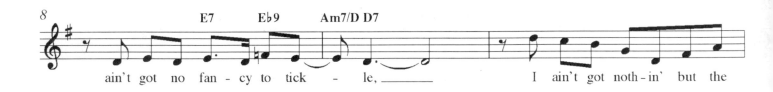

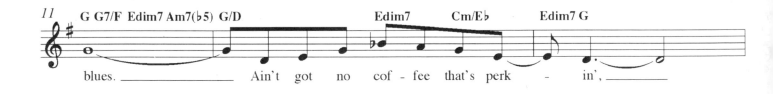

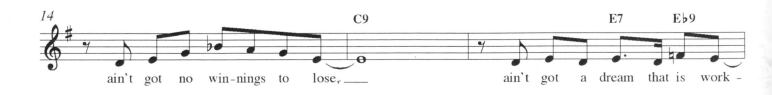

When trum - pets flare up _____ I keep my hair up, —

I just can't make it come down. — Be - lieve me,

pap - py, _____ I can't get hap - py — since my ev - er-lov - in' ba - by left town. —

_____ Ain't got no rest on my slum - - - bers. _____

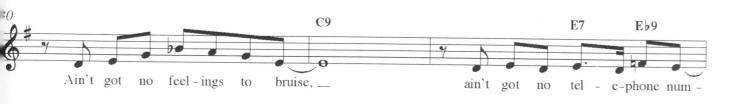

Ain't got no feel - ings to bruise, __ ain't got no tel - e-phone num -

- - bers, _____ I ain't got noth - in' but the blues.

Ain't got the change of a nick - blues. _____

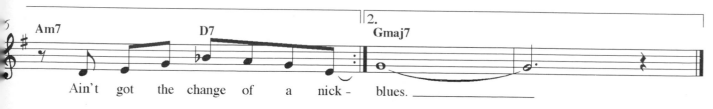

I'll Be Seeing You

Bb Instruments

Music by Sammy Fain
Lyric by Irving Kahal

Moderately

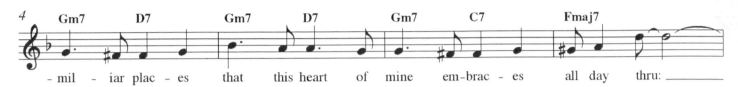

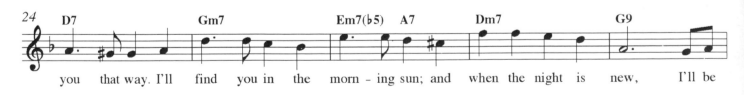

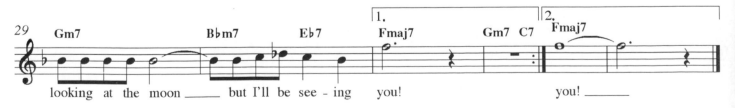

I'm Beginning To See The Light

B♭ Instruments

Lyric and Music by
Duke Ellington, Don George, Harry James and Johnny Hodges

It All Depends On You

Bb Instruments

Lyric and Music by B. G. DeSylva
Lew Brown and Ray Henderson

Moderately

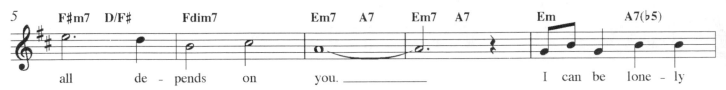

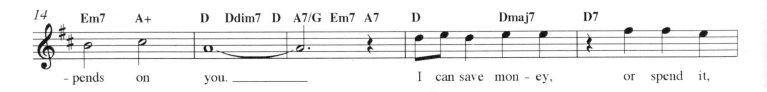

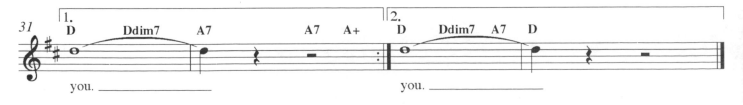

It Had To Be You

B♭ Instruments

Music by Isham Jones
Lyric by Gus Kahn

I've Got The World On A String

B♭ Instruments

Lyric by Ted Koehler
Music by Harold Arlen

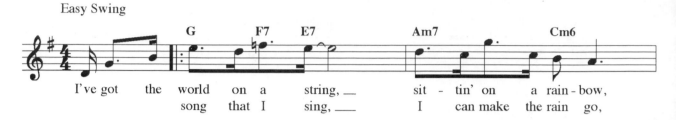

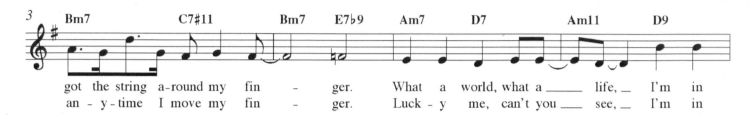

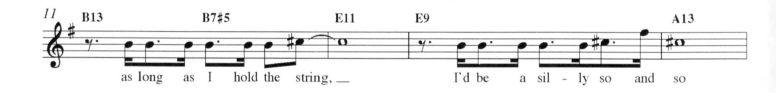

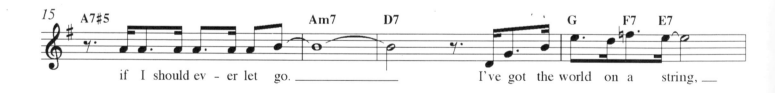

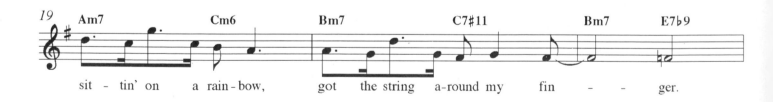

Let's Stay Together

B♭ Instruments

Lyric and Music by
Al Green, Willie Mitchell and Al Jackson, Jr.

Mood Indigo

B♭ Instruments

Lyric and Music by
Duke Ellington, Barney Bigard and Irving Mills

Moonlight In Vermont

B♭ Instruments

Lyric and Music by
John Blackburn and Karl Svessdorf

My Buddy

Bb Instruments

Music by Walter Donaldson
Lyric by Gus Kahn

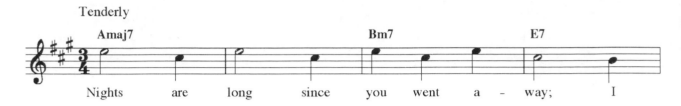

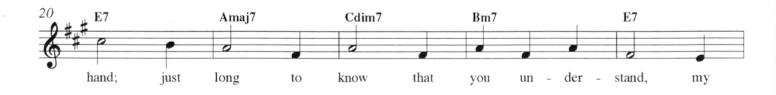

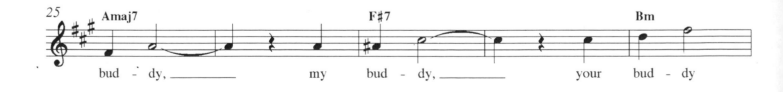

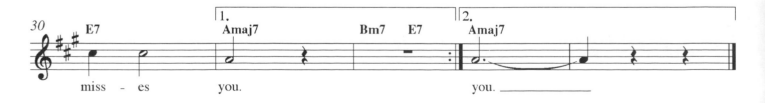

Perdido

B♭ Instruments

Music by Juan Tizol
Lyric by Ervin Drake and Hans Lengsfelder

Shiny Stockings

B♭ Instruments

Music by Frank Foster
Lyric by Ella Fitzgerald

Sweet And Lovely

Bb Instruments

Lyric and Music by Gus Arnheim,
Charles N. Daniels and Harry Tobias

Stormy Weather
(Keeps Rainin' All The Time)

B♭ Instruments

Music by Harold Arlen
Lyric by Ted Koehler

Slow

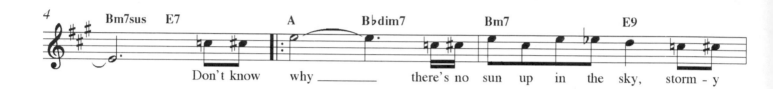

Don't know why _____ there's no sun up in the sky, storm - y

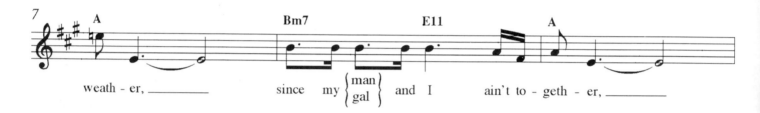

weath - er, _____ since my { man } { gal } and I ain't to - geth - er, _____

keeps rain - in' all ___ the time. _____ Life is

bare, _____ gloom and mis - 'ry ev - 'ry-where, storm - y weath - er, _____

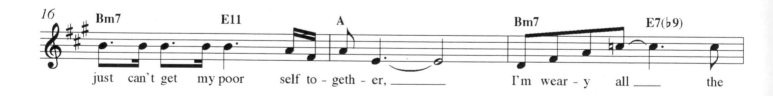

just can't get my poor self to - geth - er, _____ I'm wear - y all ___ the

time. _____ The time, _____ so wear - y all ___ the time. _____

Stormy weather 2-2

Taking A Chance On Love

Bb Instruments

Lyric by John LaTouche & Ted Fetter
Music by Vernon Duke

Here I go a-gain. __ I hear those trum-pets blow a-gain. __

All a-glow a-gain, __ tak-ing a chance on love.

Here I slide a-gain, __ a-bout to take that ride a-gain. __

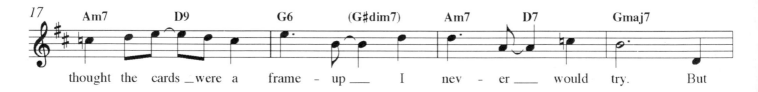

Star-ry eyed a-gain, __ tak-ing a chance on love. I

thought the cards __ were a frame-up __ I nev-er __ would try. But

now I'm tak-ing the game up __ and the ace of hearts is high.

Things are mend-ing now. __ I see a rain-bow bend-ing now. __

We'll have our hap-py end-ing now, __ tak-ing a chance on love.

Teach Me Tonight

B♭ Instruments

Lyric by Sammy Cahn
Music by Gene DePaul

That Sunday, That Summer

B♭ Instruments

Lyric and Music by
George David Weiss and Joe Sherman

There Will Never Be Another You

B♭ Instruments

Lyric by Mack Gordon
Music by Harry Warren

Lyrics:

There will be man-y oth-er nights like this, _____ and I'll be stand-ing here with some-one new, _____ There will be oth-er songs to sing, an-oth-er fall, an-oth-er spring, but there will nev-er be an-oth-er you. _____ There will be oth-er lips that I may kiss, _____ but they won't thrill me like yours used to do, _____ yes, I may dream a mil-lion dreams, but how can they come true, if there will nev-er ev-er be an-oth-er you? There you?

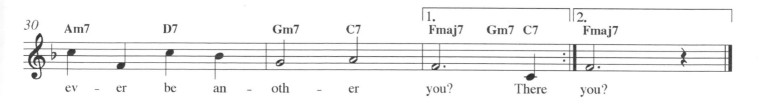

'Tis Autumn

B♭ Instruments

Lyric and Music by
Henry Nemo

Too Close For Comfort

B♭ Instruments

Lyric and Music by
George David Weiss, Jerry Bock
and Lawrence Holofcener

We'll Be Together Again

Bb Instruments

Lyric by Frankie Laine
Music by Carl Fischer

What Now My Love?

B♭ Instruments

Music by Gilbert Becaud
English Lyric by Carl Sigman
French Lyric by Perre Leroyer

When Lights Are Low

Bb Instruments

Lyric by Spencer Williams
Music by Benny Carter

Medium Slow Jazz

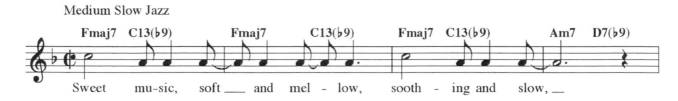

Sweet mu-sic, soft ___ and mel - low, sooth - ing and slow, ___

strains of a mel - low cel - lo, when lights are low. ___

Dear, we're so close ___ to - geth - er, I love you so. ___

Why think a - bout ___ the wea - ther when lights are low? ___

Two hearts re - veal - ing, ___ mu - sic hath charms. ___

Life's so ap - peal - ing with in - spi - ra - tion in ___ your arms. ___ Our

lips meet-ing soft ___ and ten - der, love's all a - glow. ___

Why should-n't we ___ sur - ren - der when lights are low? ___

When You're Smiling
(The Whole World Smiles With You)

B♭ Instruments

Lyric and Music by
Mark Fisher, Joe Goodwin and Larry Shay

Where Are You?

Bb Instruments

Music by Jimmy McHugh
Lyric by Harold Adamson

Where Do I Begin
(Theme From The Motion Picture "Love Story")

Bb Instruments

Lyric by Carl Sigman
Music by Francis Lai

You Were Meant For Me

B♭ Instruments

Lyric and Music by
Jewel Kilcher and Steve Poltz

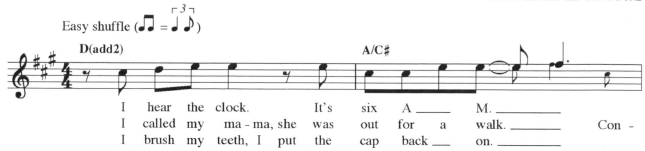

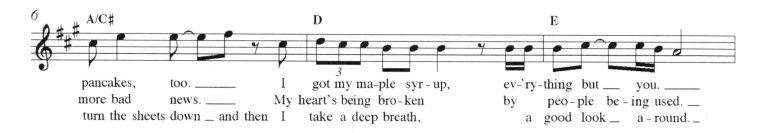

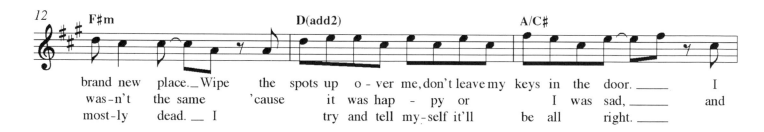

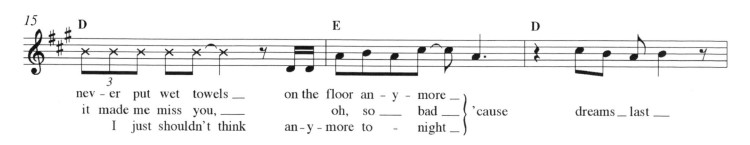

You Go To My Head

B♭ Instruments

Music by J. Fred Coots
Lyric by Haven Gillespie